Tayler Lewis

The heroic Periods in a Nation's History

An Appeal to the Soldiers of the American Armies

Tayler Lewis

The heroic Periods in a Nation's History
An Appeal to the Soldiers of the American Armies

ISBN/EAN: 9783337133641

Printed in Europe, USA, Canada, Australia, Japan

Cover: Foto ©ninafisch / pixelio.de

More available books at **www.hansebooks.com**

THE

HEROIC PERIODS

IN

A NATION'S HISTORY.

AN APPEAL TO THE SOLDIERS OF THE AMERICAN ARMIES.

BY

TAYLER LEWIS,

UNION COLLEGE.

NEW YORK:
BAKER & GODWIN, PRINTERS,
PRINTING-HOUSE SQUARE.
1866.

ADDRESS.

A NATION is born, a league is made. The one is a natural and historical product, the other an outward and artificial construction. The one has an inward organic power making its organization what it is, the other is made by its organization as a purely outward adjustment. In other words, a nation has a true life, vivifying every part, and felt in every part; a league is a mere balance of power, an equilibrium of mechanical forces. Hence a nation has a true political personality; it has a conscience, an accountability; a league is the creature of diplomacy: it can have, at the highest, no other principle for its inward or outward action than a time-serving expediency; there can enter in its history no high question of right, for anything of the kind would be a disturbing instead of a conserving element. A nation claims a true allegiance; a league has no higher obligation than a temporary contract, which each party may put an end to, with no other consideration than its own safety in so doing. A nation is an historical power ordained of God, and representing God upon earth; a league is a purely human thing, a contrivance of politicians, often the lowest contrivance of the lowest politicians. Such political alliances have often appeared in history. There were the ever-dissolving Grecian confederacies; there was the short-lived Achaean league, the best of them all; there were the Italian leagues of the middle ages; there have been European congresses and alliances of more modern times; going back into the remote past, we find the remarkable "confederacy," mentioned by the Psalmist, of "Edom and the Ishmaelites, of Moab and the Hargarenes;" last of all there has been the Southern Confederacy, beginning to crumble as soon as formed, having the elements of weakness and wickedness in its very inception, and falling to pieces through its own innate depravity, its own inbred dissensions, even when a fierce outward conflict was giving it an unnatural vigor and an artificial enthusiasm. It might have destroyed the nation whose life it assailed; it never could have sustained itself. Its brief wretched existence shows us the fearful danger we have all escaped, the fatal wreck that might have come over the whole nation, from the example even of its temporary success.

Political combinations of this kind have ever exhibited the same base features. Products of an evil diplomacy were they all. Their history is nothing but a history of faction and intrigue. They have ever presented the worst aspects of human nature, destroying social integrity, and weakening the sense of obligation in the individual man, by merging it in a soulless mechanism having neither life, nor honor, nor conscience, nor accountability. They have never had anything great and glorious about them, except as they have approached, or been transformed into, the national idea, or have had a transient honor from flashes of glory that have occasionally appeared in some of their component parts. In themselves, they have ever been the deformities of human history. For such leagues there are no elements of the sublime, because there are no necessary historical ideas connected with them; no elevating reminiscences of the past; no proud hopes of the future: no inspiring eras; no symbolic words and days to call out a lofty enthusiasm; no great questions of right; in a word, no heroic periods, such as are ever associated with the ideas of a true political personality, and of a precious national life. All is sordid, low, selfish. Such political mechanisms, if they deserve the name, may be said to have, in truth, no history in themselves, or as wholes. It is simply a record of the selfish, sectional struggles of the parts with each other and with the

embracing combination. This must be so, since there is no
national feeling—in other words, no feeling of a common life,
to prevent it. The annals of such a soulless corporation can
give us nothing more than the unceasing strivings of sections
ever disturbing in the very effort to maintain this mechanical
balance of power, or ever seeking to separate themselves from
the merely artificial whole with which they are connected by
no living bond.

It is only a nation that can have anything truly heroic in
its history, and the converse of this holds equally true; every
real nation created by God, even the smallest and most
obscure of them, have had, somewhere in the course of their
political existence, their heroic periods. It is the historical
sign of nationality. It has been their birth struggle, or some
other eventful time or times to which they are ever looking back,
as that which gives them a title to stand in the family of nations. It is that which gave them oneness and totality, or secured it against destruction, and to which they, therefore,
refer as identical with their national life and national continuance. Even Portugal thus looks back to the days of Vasco
da Gama; Holland remembers, and yet lives in, the remembrance of her glorious struggle for nationality; and so, too,
the national existence of Sweden yet derives strength from
the great period of her emerging from anarchy in the days of
Gustavus Vasa. It is the remembrance of Tell and his heroic
time that makes Switzerland a true nation, preventing the league
character, which enters too much into her structure, from
wholly marring her noble history. In the greater nations
this has shown itself still more strikingly. All that is politically high and glorious has ever connected itself with these
thoughts of a national life, as a true personality having at
some periods of its course such facts of a glorious past, and
making that past the ground of its hope in the future.

A heroic age may be briefly defined as one predominantly
unselfish, or as a time when the self-consciousness, both
individual and national, is all taken up in some strong absorb-

1*

ing emotion—when a strange elevation of feeling and corresponding dignity of action are seen in men, and they seem to
be carried on by impulses that appear extravagant to the more
calculating temperaments of succeeding times. This heroic
spirit is not grace, nor religion, but that which stands next to
them among the moving powers of humanity. It is, in other
words, the highest thing purely human. Strong feeling, like
the pure reason, is unselfish, and the heroism of which we
speak may be characterized as the self-forgetfulness aroused by
a great *right*, or a great *idea*, and grounded on the fact that
the ideal in man is ever higher and purer than his ordinary
actual. The denial of this is a mere play upon words. It is
enough to justify the name that such intense passion, so called
out, is something far above the low, sordid, consciously calculating selfishness of our common life. Such heroic periods in
a nation's history seemed designed by Providence, not for
themselves only, or the great effects of which they are the
immediate causes, but for their influence upon the whole after-
current of the national existence. The strong remembrance
becomes a part of the national life ; it enters afterward into
the common and constant thinking ; it gives a peculiar direction to the national feeling; it imparts a higher character to
its subsequent action ; it makes the whole historical being
very different from what it would have been had there been no
such epic commencement, no such heroic time or times. It fur-
nishes a treasury of glorious reminiscences wherewith to rein-
vigorate the national virtue when impaired, as it is so like to
be, by the factions, and selfish, and unheroic temper produced
by subsequent days of merely economical or utilitarian prosperity.

And thus *we* stand in the family of nations. Young as
we are we too have had our heroic periods, the second, in
respect to glory, every way worthy of being named together
with the first. The earlier struggle has passed into history,
and its character is secured. The critical after-period was
marked by no compromises, no letting down of the heroic

idea out of a false charity to traitors, no belittling of the great struggle, no marring of its honor by any attempts to give equal honor to its domestic foes, no obscuring the great truth for the political accommodation of tories who had fought against it, no yielding the great right by admitting to its equal guardianship men who had zealously opposed its assertion, no sinking into ignominy the whole contest, on both sides, by lessening that great right to a mere question of "standpoints," as though it had in itself no intrinsic, unchangeable truth as seen from every stand-point. The men of that day never admitted that they went through a long and fierce war to settle what might have at any time been viewed as an open question, or which had not been regarded as irrevocably decided from the beginning. They fought not to *settle* what was in itself doubtful, and which, therefore, never could be so settled, but to *assert* and *maintain* what was certain, vital, never to be yielded. Such was the temper of the men who essayed the "reconstruction" of our nation after the war in which it had its birth. No such proceedings followed our first glorious epoch as now threaten to tarnish the lustre of the second and to deprive it of all its due historic effect.

It is all idle for the false conservative to say that there is no danger of this. History does, indeed, in time, assert itself, and the value of the heroic is not wholly lost, but it may be obscured for generations. There never was for England a nobler period than that of the wars of the Puritans against the Stuarts. Its honor is now again emerging from the cloud, but we know that unprincipled reaction and a base reconstruction, under the name of restoration, put the brand of inglorious centuries upon the most heroic cause and the most heroic names in English history. We must see to it that our Hampdens, our Pyms, and our Vanes, our civil and military heroes, our glorious asserters of the fundamental idea of the American Republic be not suffered to fall under the same long reproach. Above all must we see to it that the Monks and the

Clarendons do not get the upper hand—that *they* be not the men to represent us and our history in generations to come.

There is no need to dwell further on our first great historical time. Another similar epoch, still more terrible, is yet to have its place and character assigned to it. It is not too much to say that we are now assigning it. This present political canvass is to determine whether the conflict through which we have just passed is to take its place of honor beside our first struggle, and to go down to history in company with it, or whether it is to be stripped, for a time at least, of all its grander features, and reckoned among the inglorious wars of faction, differing in no respect from a vulgar prize-fight except in the ocean of bloodshed which it has occasioned.

A war of faction, a bloody mob-fight growing out of a presidential election, a base contest between "two sets of extremists," each equally wrong, equally deserving the reprobation of the country—an ignominious strife, "swinging round from South to North;" such is the representation given by Andrew Johnson, when he himself revives again these words of faction, the North and the South—talking of extremists when, in all the proceedings that for long years were preparing this war, he himself was one of the extremes of Southern extremists, voting with them through Kansas, through Lecompton, his name standing on record with Davis, Mason, Slidell, Tombs, and Wigfall, as constantly and as regularly as the letters of the alphabet. He now sees things "swinging round," and puts on a par with the extremists to whom he had so long allied himself (even to the very verge of the traitorous plunge) men who never violated a law of the land, and who have been ever foremost in defense of our national honor.

So, Seward calls it "a civil war," as other advocates of the rebellion have compared it to the American revolution. Between this and the unspeakable crime of the Southern leaders there is no parallel whatever. Besides being for a most righteous cause, our first war with Britain was a contest between a mother country and a far-distant misgoverned colony. It differed in no essential aspect from a war b-tween two distant nations. It was a separation coming in the natural course of things, as belonging to the very intent and idea of colonization. As compared with the Southern war for slavery, it presents all the difference between the necessary pains of parturition and the most foul matricidal murder. In like manner, Seward's deceptive term, a "civil war," is equally out of place. It is designed to lower the whole struggle, even as the other comparison was meant unduly to elevate the South. But it is an utter misnomer. It was no civil war. This term is rightly applied to contentions where two opposing forces in a state are striving in an irregular and violent manner for the mastery, neither seeking to destroy the nation, but each, on the contrary, protesting their superior devotion to the preservation of the national life. Such wars have been frequent in the world, disastrous and bloody, though not wholly destitute, on both sides, of some features of the heroic. Such were in England the wars of the Roses; such were the struggles between King and Parliament. They were not like this indescribable rebellion against republicanism. So France, too, can find redeeming elements of glory in her fierce revolutions. For in none of these contests was either French or English nationality ever assailed. Neither party thought of harming it. All would have united in a struggle for its preservation, one and indivisible. The Cromwellian and the cavalier, the aristocrat and the sans culottes, held alike sacred that precious historical idea on which we have insisted as the radical distinction between a nation and a base, factious league. But in our own case how utterly the reverse was the spectacle presented! It was the very life of the nation that was assailed; it was an effort by the foulest means to blot it out of history. This was the unspeakable crime attempted by the plotting "extremists" with whom Andrew Johnson had been so long connected. For this there were sought the basest foreign alliances. This vile league had its still viler leagues abroad. Recreant to the name and the idea of republicanism, they had their emissaries praying aid from European monarchies, not in defense of, but for the destruction of, the freest and most beneficent government on earth. Men who once sat in the Senate of the United States, men with whose ayes and noes Andrew Johnson's voice had long sounded in unbroken unison, lurking at foreign courts where the very name of their country was hateful and her noble institutions of freedom were more dreaded than anything else on earth! This was the utterly un-American proceeding of the Southern Confederacy ; this was the unspeakable crime of Mason and Slidell, whom Andrew Johnson would compare with Wilson, and Andrews, and Sumner, and Fenton, and Stevens, and Curtin, "at the other end of the line." What crimes have "these men" committed that they should be so stigmatized? What have they done except to defend, most ably and manfully, opinions which, whether we call them practical or not, every man knows to be in soul-accordance with the Declaration of Independence, in most *conservative* harmony with that great historical document which underlies all our republican ideas, and gives us our distinctive character among the nations of the earth. For long years had Andrew Johnson's colleagues freely maintained opinions subversive of all these ideas, though holding, all the time, the highest offices in the government. But "these men," whose only excess, if it be excess, is in their love of freedom—"these men" the President calls the Northern traitors. At every railway station the same violent language is repeated. He means by this the unbroken loyal party, including Congress and the governors of all the loyal States. He means by it just what copperhead editors have meant by the same language throughout the war. But strangest sight of all is what may be called the afterpiece in this dramatic performance. At every repetition, forth steps one who was for so many years an honored leader in this party, one who gained the name of its chief " radical " from those who now assail it. He has no confession to make, but hardly is the intemperate harangue concluded when he appears upon the railway stage and blandly says: This is all just so, my fellow-citizens;—what our great and good President tells you is nothing but the honest truth. Could there well be conceived a more melancholy spectacle? And yet we would not forget the great services that this man has rendered to the cause of right and freedom. We will rather tax our fancy to invent palliations for his present course, than to believe that in the past days of his high and deserved renown he was either self-ignorant or insincere. It was not merely aid that these Southern "extremists" sought; they endeavored to degrade, in every possible way, the republic which Washington and Franklin had helped to found. They continually cast the foulest reproach upon our history and our name. Men now seeking admission to Congress, men lately sitting in the Johnson-Philadelphia Convention, were foremost in the planning and the execution of these base anti-national embassies. A civil war might have been waged and yet each party preserve an American and a republican position. A civil war, had it been truly such, might have had a ground for conciliation; this utterly traitorous and un-American proceeding excludes every idea of harmonious action with the guilty participants. The men who did this, the men who planned and supported it, may have an amnesty consigning them to contempt, though leaving to them life and property; they may have mercy with ignominy, but forgiveness never. We mean national and political forgiveness. They can never more be permitted to sit in an American senate; they can never more be trusted with the national honor. This sinks as they rise; the cause for which 250,000 men have died loses its historical glory just in proportion as these men are suffered to emerge from their infamy.

"Our late civil war," says Secretary Seward. By such language as this he would seem to regard it, not as a struggle for a nation's life, but a party fight, to be cured by a little diplomacy. The "higher law" was forgotten in his pleasant chat with Governor Perry about "Northern and Southern standpoints." It all became a matter of perspective. The "irrepressible conflict" resolved itself into a difference of latitude, a mere difference of style, according as a speech happened to be made in Charleston or New York. A fight between two parties! Most true, indeed, but who were the parties? Everything depends upon the right naming of the issue. It was not North and South. It was not two factions *in* a nation, each equally zealous, or professing to be, for nationality. It was the *Nation* versus *Rebels*. It was the nation on the one side, the whole nation, in its total political idea, a republican nation, with its national life, struggling with men North and South who were seeking to destroy that life, to bury the national idea, and resorting to the most unscrupulous as well as the most bloody means to effect their purpose.

It is here that the distinction we have made becomes of vital importance, and that is the reason why we have so strongly insisted upon it. It at once clears up the issue and exposes the deceptive statement. Had we been a mere league, there might have been some more plausible ground for characterizing it as such a factious "civil war." It was, on the other hand, the nation warring with a most mischievous idea that long had been poisoning its vitality, and which could only save its life by casting it out. It was not secession merely—a thing which may be asserted or renounced according to the expediencies of the times—but that from which secession inevitably comes. It was, we say again, a nation contending for its life. What must we think of a man making high claims to the reputation of a statesman who could overlook or ignore this vital point. It was not North versus South, nor even States against States; that view is the product of the disorganizing league idea. Even in these rebellious States the nation existed all along—as much in Georgia as in New York. It never ceased for a moment to be present in every part during the hottest period of the war, the same as before and after it. In all these seceding portions there had been, for eighty years, the high national jurisdiction, superior to, yet in concurrence with, the local, and that, too, not as a government over States (as that of States over individuals), or coming in contact with the individual only by means of State intervention, but reaching down through the States, exercising direct jurisdiction, having direct power over, and claiming direct allegiance from, every man, black or white, included in their lower geographical organizations. This national jurisdiction was never lost, never relaxed. It was at no time a mere waiting claim, or in any manner put in abeyance, but insisted upon, and enforced every moment by the most vigorous action, until fully and triumphantly reasserted. Mr. Lincoln's oath, "registered in heaven," never lost for a moment the solemnity and the power of its sublime attestation. As became inevitable in such a conflict, the opposing local governments perished—perished by the very position in which they had placed themselves—perished by their own suicidal acts. Unless we hold that death may be a part of life, or that disorganization may be the law of an organic structure, or that a thing may be at the same time in violent resistance and yet in harmonious relation to the whole of which it forms a constituent portion, the conclusion must follow: The State governments, taking this position, perished; but the nation never lost, never loosed its hold. This is not metaphysics but common sense. Whatever ideal States may have remained hidden away, and out of all sight of the actual, as some have dreamed, the assumed State governments of which McGrath, and Vance, and Letcher claimed to be heads, were not States that the nation could acknowledge; for a State is an organization, a lawful organization, and not a mere geographical space, or a collection of people. They ceased to be States—States in the Union, and we can know no other. The lower perished, but the "higher law" lived on; the national jurisdiction survived amid all the tumult, and when the struggle ended this was the only political vitality left unharmed in these rebellious portions. As such it was the fountain, the only fountain, of any future vitality, of any future political organization for these disorgan-

2

ized communities. The nation still remained unbroken, "un-impaired;" and it was the nation, through its legislative body constitutionally representing it in such action, that could alone re-tore the lower and the lost jurisdiction. From it new life must flow to those broken, and wasted, and withered members of the body politic. Here resided the *vis medicatrix* from which alone could come the healing power. For four years there had been no governors in those States, no legislatures, no judicial officers whom the nation could acknowledge There was not one among them who had taken the national oath essential to the validity of their action. It was not a partial severance, a partial disorder, that might be cured by partial order yet remaining. The tie of allegiance was broken everywhere and in all. There was no political or official soundness of any kind, whatever remains of loyalty might be found, here and there, in individuals. All was anarchy. There was no beginning *de novo* from themselves. No part, no class, had any more right to make any such commencement than another. There was no *convening* power, and hence, there could be no lawfully acknowledged *conventions*. There was, in short, no law there except this higher law, which had never perished. There was nothing to determine franchise, or when or how such franchise should be exercised. The rebel governor, the rebel legislature, the rebel genera's, had no more power here than the rebel soldier in the ranks, certainly not more than the persecuted unionist, or the loyal colored man. A military authority might, in the meantime, keep the peace; but the nation, through its once concurrent and never lost jurisdiction, the nation as legislatively represented, could alone reorganize. Every other view lands us in contradiction and absurdity, or would compel us to admit the lawfulness of continued revolution as an escape from the difficulty. Ignoring the only remaining fountain of law and right, we must leave the whole question of future political life to the mere chances of anarchy, with the expectation of something in some way turning up that might afterward be made regular by the national acknowledgment. But then it would not be the same old State, but a new one, arising in an anarchical and revolutionary manner; for there could be no continuance of the old life but through some life remaining, and that, as we have shown, was the unbroken national jurisdiction, once concurrent, but now exclusive, because it is all that remains to make a beginning, however that which is thus begun might be left (after full restoration) to the old power of changing its constitution as it pleased, and with no other restriction than a truly republican form, in harmony with the Constitution of the nation. This alone could bridge the chasm of anarchy and revolution; for law, as distinguished from these, is a living thing, a continuous energy, and not a mere arrangement of dead expediencies. Hence such a course is no less a *necessity* for the dismembered parts, than it is the high *right* of the nation; for lawful organizations can only proceed regularly from organizations previously existing, regarded as initiating and regulating the inceptive modes of those that follow. Especially does this living power of law find its highest exemplification in republican governments, whose beauty and perfection it is that the greatest flexibility and diversity may be secured without those chasms and convulsions that are sometimes rendered necessary under other forms. *The power of restoring, reconstructing, initiating into political life the broken members, resides in the unbroken national whole.* That settled, one question only yet remains: who represent the nation in this, the executive or the law-making power, that is, Congress, together with the President, so far as by his veto he rightfully performs a legislative act. That question we will not here argue. Had it not been for late events, it seems difficult to imagine how any doubt could possibly have arisen in respect to the one and only answer to be given by any rational mind. All this might be argued from the very idea of nationality in its bearing on the case before us. But it has not been left to abstract reasoning. The express provision that Congress, as thus legislatively representing the nation, shall guarantee to each State a republican form of government, puts the matter at rest. It is difficult to imagine a case to which it is more perfectly applicable than that of a State that has broken its relations to the Union, and lost its true position by rebellion. In ordinary times it would seem like a provision for whose application no emergency could arise. The great men who framed the Constitution are not known to have anticipated any such terrible convulsion as that through which we have passed; and their having so perfectly provided for it, therefore, may well warrant the reverent belief that in this most essential article they were wisely and providentially guided by "One who loved our nation."

In reviewing this argument we are carried back to that most vital distinction, before insisted upon, between a nation and a league. It at once resolves the wretched sophism of *in* and *out* by which our most illogical President, and his no less illogical Secretary, have so complicated the great measure and the great question of the day. A certain class of reasoners are ever fond of what the technical logicians call the dilemma. It is so easy apparently. They can turn it in almost any way to suit any application, and in doing this they seem to be unconscious how easily it may be turned directly against them. A State, say these astute logicians, is either *in* the Union or it is *out*, or if it is not *in*, then it is *out*. If it is *out*, then secession has been successful. We fought four years, and lost so many lives in denial of the doctrine that a State could go *out*, and now "the radicals" say they actually *were* out, and that, therefore, legislation is necessary to bring them in again, etc., etc. There are many men who really regard this as an argument; and how conclusive they think it is shown by the great use that was made of it by Democrats and so-called Conservatives in Congress. It is hard to deal patiently with such a wretched quibble. The clear mind of Lincoln saw through it intuitively. His distinction between a perfect position in, and a disordered relation to, the Union is only a presentation, in other terms, of the two ideas on which we have been dwelling. The bare statement solves at once the boasted dilemma. These rebellious States were *out* of the *Union*, but they were never out of the *Nation;* they were not permitted to be, they never shall be permitted to be *out* of the *Nation*. They were out of the *union*, which, important as it is, is not the nation, but the *form* of the nation, the organization of the nation, or rather the form of its organization. This is what Mr. Lincoln meant by saying they were out of relation, out of their practical order in the nation. But they were never out of the Nation itself, as something lying back of the union, older than the union, and that *made the union*, when it said, " We, the people, do ordain and establish." They were never out of that God-formed political entity, that great historical power the substantial being, the very *substance* itself, lying under and back of all *forms*, and whence all conventional, political forms derive their power and their only lawful being. They broke the Constitution, and have, therefore, no right to name it in their defense ; but they never broke the Nation that *made the Constitution*. To return to Mr. Seward's statement of the issue, it was this nation, one and indivisible, that was the grand party of the first part in the great contest through which we have passed. The other party may have any name, or names, that any may choose to give it. We may call them mobs or states, as we please, or we may say it was a warring with an antinational idea, upheld by mobs and States, and which the national life required to be cast out at all hazards. It was not a fight between two sets of extremists, "swinging round," as Andrew Johnson says; that is simply a degradation of the whole matter. It was not a war between North and South, it was not a war between two factions in a nation, it was not a civil war. All these paltry ideas belittle the contest, and dishonor the mighty hosts of the dead. It was a nation, we say again, struggling for its life. It was the nation against rebels at the South and malignant copperheads at the North, combined with all in Europe who desired our ruin, who were oppofed to the glorious doctrine of human brotherhood, and who hated the very name of republicanism.

There is a third method of belittleing the great cause. It takes the form of chivalry. It talks of honorable foes. It affects to doubt whether treason has really been committed; and if it has been, treason, it says, is no dishonorable crime; as though there were no difference between a war of aristocratic factions in a monarchy and this long-plotted, assassin-like assault upon a nation's life—between rebellion against the " divine right of kings " and such a diabolical attempt to destroy the divine right to live of the noblest republican government on earth, and that, too, by open complicity with its most deadly foreign foes. In promoting this phase of reaction, Mr. Montgomery Blair is the chief agent. He would almost give the palm of heroism to the rebellion. They were at least equally heroic, equally patriotic in their way, and now that the prize-fight is over, equally entitled to come in and share in the future legislation of the country. Some who lived in the more immediate vicinity of this rebellious pestilence still hold precious the national idea. It was with them stronger than the sectional feeling, which the league doctrine, and Blair's interpretation of it, would make the predominant and the higher principle. Those brave men who perilled all in the cause of loyalty and nationality were "recreants," forsooth, to the chivalrous, though, perhaps, mistaken spirit of the greater numbers around them. The speaker would seem to have forgotten that Andrew Johnson once claimed to be one of this very class; but no language could have more clearly shown how far this Johnsonian movement, in its " swinging round," has receded from the spirit which actuated the nation when Sherman marched through South Carolina.

According to Blair, there was really no high and immutable principle involved. It was a mere matter of " stand-points." The rebels, from their position, had some claim to the allegiance of those around them. Notwithstanding the contempt they were endeavoring to bring upon everything American and republican, they were still, for the South, the chivalrous party, the patriotic party, and those suffering adherents to the national idea were "recreants." The other side were fighting for their honor, the honor of their women—how perfectly has he learned the false rebel cant—they were "repelling assailants!" How dare this "recreant," whom Lincoln once trusted—how dare he thus defame the martyr's memory, the honor of the loyal living, and of the heroic dead! With him it is a mere shifting of position in the examination of a picture. They, from their "stand-point," viewed it so and so, and they were "honorable men." We, from our stand-point, viewed it somewhat differently, and we, too, are honorable men ; we are all honorable men. In this wretched attempt to save the sectional honor, and to revive, for new party purposes, the sectional spirit, how irretrievably sinks the national honor, and with it the honor of the countless dead! As one side of the scale here rises, the other inevitably falls. Think of it, soldiers, for your glory is deeply involved in that of the cause for which you fought. They must go down in history together. Think of it, for the honor of your dead comrades, when the solemn question comes up, "Who slew all these?" We are more concerned in these awful words than were they to whom the avenging Jehu anciently addressed them. This vast slaughter? We are now deciding the question whether it was indeed a great *right*, a great idea, involving a nation's life, that demanded such a sacrifice, or whether it was what the Blair and Seward representation would make it to be, the foulest as well as the most inexcusable national crime that history has ever recorded. This is the question, soldiers, and your votes are to determine to which of the political tendencies now drawing in such diametrically opposite directions, the nation's honor, and your honor, may most safely be confided. To see this clearly is to determine at once how you shall vote.

Nothing can be more evident than that in all such language as held by Blair and Seward there is a virtual denial of there having been ever any great question of right and truth involved in the contest. They may not wish so to present it, but the necessities of the new Johnson movement drive them inevitably toward it. There was then no "higher law," there was no "irrepressible conflict of ideas," demanding such a burthen of national debt, and such a holocaust of heroic lives. No ideas have been changed by it. We are again as we were. To meet the new party emergency secession even must be mildly treated. It must be represented as having been, once at least, an open question, with the inevitable conclusion that if so, it is an open question still, whenever there is again the strength and the opportunity for its assertion; for force can never settle right; and war should only be for the *maintenance* of an undoubted right, not to *settle* what was ever fairly open to dispute. Besides, the future Orrs, and Hamptons, and Monroes, may not feel concluded by declarations made in a Philadelphia convention. An open question once whether we were a nation or not! Eighty years of national existence had not proved it; if so, it is open yet, we say, and so is the American doctrine of political equality, and the religious doctrine of the One Humanity. Men could hold offices and take the most solemn oaths for more than half a century, and yet honestly and honorably hold that such acts created no allegiance, that such oaths made no solemn and binding obligation. They ask to swear again, or even think it ungenerous to require such a test of their present and future loyalty! They put themselves upon their right. Though the war, like a vulgar pugilistic conflict, has decided for the moment which is the stronger, yet in the beginning there was little or no difference of principle. It was a factious dispute, leading to a most bloody issue; but we were all about equally right, equally wrong, equally honorable, each equally entitled to come and with " unimpaired rights " share in the future government. In the name of the dead, we protest against a doctrine so utterly demoralizing, both politically and morally, as this. Blessed are the merciful, but truth and right before all things. Holy is charity, but we debase the name; we hold up instead of it a vile,

lying thing, worse in the sight of God than an honest vindic-
tiveness, when we forget that charity rejoiceth in the truth.
An open question! or one that might fairly seem such!
What right had we from the Eternal Justice to settle, in this
awfully bloody way an open question, or even one so doubtful
that it might be rationally disputed? How had we been
lying to the world for eighty years, if the question of our
American nationality had been open, or even controvertible!
If there was not, on the side of the nation, a clear right, a
great right, a most holy and indispensable right—a right
which could not be waived at any hazard—then our war was
a great national crime, and every man concerned in it, from
the highest to the lowest, from the commander-in-chief to the
poorest soldier in the ranks, ought to humble himself and con-
fess the sin of his participation. Above all, how must it come
home to the conscience of one who now takes this estimate of
it, who now calls it a mere civil war, yet who may be charged,
if this view be a correct one, with having done more to bring
on a strife so bloody, yet so causeless, than any single individual at the North! With heart-felt sorrow do we say this
of an old friend and classmate. We appeal from William
H. Seward of 1866 to William H. Seward of 1856—from his
talk with Governor Perry of South Carolina to his speeches in
the days of Kansas and Le Compton—from his low position
now to his lofty position then. He was not mistaken. There
was such a "higher law," however he may have fallen from it.
There was that "irrepressible conflict" of ideas which he
would now merge in the lower notion of a factious strife, as a
prelude to a factious "civil war." Those to whom he held
this lofty language stand now where they did then, their ranks
unbroken, their enthusiasm for the right undiminished. He
has abandoned that great party which he described then, and
it is no less true now, as representing, more than any that had
ever existed in this country, the conscience and the intellect of
the land. If intelligence, education, morality and religion are
radicalism, they were radical then, even as a false-named con-

servatism calls them radical now. They have not changed, but he stands to-day with their opponents. He is associated now with rebels and copperheads, not honored by them, never to be trusted, never to be supported by them for any exalted station. They can never forgive his "higher law," even though he himself may seem to have renounced it.

How long shall we be fooled by platforms and resolutions made to order, instead of looking at movements, and tendencies, and affinities, whose direction cannot be mistaken, and which are the only things that leave their mark in history! The instincts that bring false men and false parties together are more unerring than our keenest reasoning. They show an invisible logic of events driving to their conclusions with more certainty than could ever be derived from any abstract argumentation. Who, for example, can mistake the nature of the movement that rallies every Northern Copperhead and Southern Rebel, pardoned or unpardoned, round Andrew Johnson, and so demands, as an assurance and a necessity of its success, this lowering of the great idea for which the nation fought, this letting down of the heroic spirit to meet its factious needs. It must sink, if they would rise. Its grand treasure of lofty reminiscences must be wasted if they would come into power. It is this lowering *tendency* that appals us more than any technical measures of reconstruction. It is a sufficient argument that those measures must be wrong that most require it. We go against that tendency, without asking any question about "the policy" connected with it. We go with that party which is most directly in the way of such a movement, without thinking of its perfection or imperfection as a party, or any charges of radicalism that may be brought against any members of it. This one fact would we keep ever before the mind : *The character of our great war is changing*, and, unless the downward tendency is arrested, will continue to change, until the movement lands us in our own demoralizing contempt, and makes true the scoffs of our enemies throughout the world.

O the dead and gone! the myriads of the slain! how keen the pang, how utterly unendurable the thought, that ye should have died in such a war as these representations would make it to be—having so litttle of principle, so little of the heroic, either in result or in idea. Ye verily thought that ye were contending for a great right, when Lo, it turns out to be a mere strife of factions "swinging round." *Your* enemies, and the enemies of republicanism, were nearly as honorable as yourselves; they had nearly, if not quite, as good grounds of right as yourselves! They were compelled to lay down their arms; they fight no longer, they have thrown up the sponge, as the vulgar boxer says, and now we must treat each other, and indulge in a mutual gabble, in the Blair style, about each other's pluck and bravery.

The great oath of Demosthenes comes again into remembrance. *Οὐ μὰ τοὺς ἐν Μαραθῶνι,**—No, by those who fell at Gettysburg, at Fort Fisher, and Mobile, it shall not be. This is declamation, it may be said. These are the catch-words of campaign orators, there is no argument in them. Be it so, and yet they are most rational tests of truth. They are signs of those most important things that we have mentioned, the movements and tendencies of the hour that to the plain common-sense of men have so much more significance than any amount of hair-splitting about platforms and policies. Mark well, soldiers, on which side in this present political canvass these yet honored names are most heartily and sponta-

---

* "No, by those who fell at Marathon, I swear!—by those who formed the battle line at Plataea,—by those who conquered in the sea fight at Salamis and Artemisium." We repeat this sublime passage from a former appeal, for we know of nothing in antiquity more applicable to the present time. Let this heroic apostrophe ring in every soldier's ear as he steps up to the ballot-box. The mere sound of it should do more to give his vote a right direction than twenty columns of such argument as is contained in the Philadelphia-Johnson Address. Marathon, Plataea, Salamis, were fought for *Panhellenia,* for ALL GREECE. Shall our late battle-fields resemble them, or shall they go down in history like the inglorious spots, all over Greece, when faction warred with faction, under the power of no higher principle than a petty "States *rights*" doctrine that for centuries made this fair portion of the world a political hell,—a warning instead of an example to the ages.

neously used, and where the least mention of them calls out the most enthusiastic applause. Go into one meeting and you will hear them resounding everywhere. They are the staple of every speaker; there is no cautious handling, no evasive shrinking, no ill-disguised fear lest they should call up hateful or disagreeable remembrances in the audience. Watch the movements of another gathering; how different the style of oratory! The burthen there, is all of taxes and high prices. What sparing mention of these glorious battle-fields, if they are mentioned at all! How poor the plaudits, how lacking in heart the cheers, even should cheers accompany their forced and heartless utterance. It cannot be otherwise. The themes into which, on the one side, there is thrown the whole soul of the speaker, are felt to be utterly out of harmony on the other, and we well know the facts of other years that have made them so. As well might the Babylonians have attempted to sing the songs of Sion, as a Democratic or a Johnson audience exhibit any real enthusiasm at the mention of these heroes and the bloody fields where they conquered. Ye remember Abraham Lincoln, soldiers. Mark where that noble martyr name is mentioned with the briefest notice, or is passed over in ominous silence, or only alluded to with reproach. In such meetings you will hear nothing said of monuments to his memory. How little, too, of Grant or Sherman, even though some would fain persuade you that those great captains are so insensible to their own military honor as to have sympathy with a movement that must inevitably reduce it in time to the level of the traitors Lee and Beauregard. Farragut is called a Democrat. We know not what his former party alliances may have been. But mark well, soldiers, and let Farragut himself mark well, where his true glory is most frequently rehearsed; where the story of his great deeds calls out the most rapturous enthusiasm, and to which side in this movement his fame may be most safely intrusted as indissolubly connected with the unimpaired honor of the cause in which he so nobly fought. There is, we say, a vast significance in this, and our military and naval heroes must be strangely blind if they fail to perceive it. The pirate Semmes, after robbing our commerce to the amount of fifty millions, not only goes unpunished but is elected to a judicial office, and may at any time, if the Philadelphia doctrine of "unimpaired rights" is true, be elected to and take his seat in Congress. The inevitable tendency of the new movement, headed by Johnson, is to put this infamous rebel and robber in the same or a similar grade of honor with Farragut, to make them both pictures in some such wretched tableau as was lately got up in Philadelphia of South Carolina and Massachusetts, with this difference, that whilst the one case presented a pitiable farce, this would be indeed a most sad and humbling reality. Such a thing could not take place, or tend to take place, without a corresponding denial of there being anything great in the cause for which either fought; and when this is done the heroism of the admiral stands no higher than that of the pirate; our country becomes a mere ring of faction, and both stand on the low level of the vulgar prize-fighter.

But what shall be done with the South, say some. Are we to remain forever two people, though we call ourselves one nation? It may be retorted that the strife of twenty previous years, bad as they were, did not do as much to make us two people as Andrew Johnson's "policy" has accomplished in the past twelve months. But we deny that there was any insuperable difficulty. There were ample materials for nationality in the South had there been statesmanship to discover and employ them. The old South, meaning by that the small oligarchy of powerful slaveholders who held to secession, and the league idea, and the mischievous local State rights in distinction from the true and vital State rights which it was the chief object of the national constitution to secure, or the right of each State and its people to the full benefits of citizenship and unimpaired republican institutions in every other State,— this old South, we say, that was ever plotting rebellion could never restored be—ought never to be restored. The attempt should

3

never have been made. This old oligarchical South was anti-national to the core, and could never have been made otherwise. The boldest ringleaders should have met the merited doom of treason, the remainder of this class, who had been all active participants in the rebellion, should have been content with their lives, and an utter exclusion from all political trust. They themselves expected no less. Now, true statesmanship would have seen at once that there must be other elements brought into the political construction of the Southern States, even had the absence of other material rendered necessary their importation. It would have seen it to be madness to attempt to bring back this old South, just as it was, with no opinion changed, and with every feeling embittered by a sense of their defeat. There was, we repeat it, ample material for this new element, if the old slave-holding power, the ever-rebellious power, had been once thoroughly put down, and, with that fact once known as fixed and irrevocable, other things had been allowed unhindered to assume their natural position, and had been favored in so doing. Their antirepublican deceivers disarmed and shut out from all hope of future political power, the miserable dupes, the poor whites, as they are called, might have been hopefully educated into true republicanism. In aid of this, there were the men who had ever been loyal, and the free colored population who, on every principle we hold politically sacred, were entitled to citizenship with all the impartial accompaniments that follow it in the case of other men. It would not have so much mattered what particular modes of reconstruction the President and Congress might have momentarily, or experimentally, adopted, if all had been in this spirit, and with this purpose so made necessary by the great peril through which the nation had passed. Aside from any question of right on the part of the colored people, our own safety demanded such new infusion of political elements, or the introduction of something that should substantially change the Southern representation. An ordinary knowledge, too, of human nature is sufficient to convince any one who makes the least claim to statesmanship, that had such a course been taken, and zealously pursued, with the whole constitutional power of the executive directed to it, the growth of a true national feeling, instead of being slow and difficult, would have been as rapid as that of the reverse spirit has been under a different treatment. It is idle to plead the want of constitutional power. In the first place, rebels had no right to name the constitution, and, secondly, in the acknowledged power of amnesty and pardon, lay the power of any condition the executive and legislative wisdom of the nation might see fit to attach to them. The greater power included the less, and in this simple statement lies the whole argument that has been so mischievously complicated. But now the great hindrance has been put back again. Instead of aiding the real suffering classes, one of which (the poor whites), though guilty, is entitled to our hearty commiseration, every effort has been directed to restore to power, " unimpaired " power (to use the Philadelphia word), the very heart of the rebellion, leaving these poor whites in the same ignorant dependence, and the white loyalists, together with the loyal colored population, to every indignity and every cruelty that baffled rage may heap upon them. " The suffering South," was one of the dominant notes sounded in the address of the late Johnson Convention. As there used, it was that most monstrous of all lies, a truth misstated and out of place. " The suffering South!" For whose benefit was this phrase used ? It was not in behalf of the murdered negroes, or the persecuted loyalists, or the miserable ignorant whites, but to procure political sympathy for the men who had been the authors of all the suffering North and South. " The South !" keeping up still that mischievous misnomer, which, for so many years, has put a wretched oligarchy of less than three hundred thousand slaveholders as a balance in the scales against a nation containing thirty millions of souls North and South ! " The suffering South !" There was weeping over the picture, it was said. The tears of Orr, of Dick Taylor, of Alexander H. Stephens, mingled with those of

Doolittle, Hendricks, Voorhes, and the extra-member, Vallandigham, for the sufferings of the South. The weeping lamentations have been taken up by Wise, in Virginia ; by Forrest, the butcher of Fort Pillow, in Memphis, and by Monroe, in New Orleans. It presents a tableau casting far into the shade that of South Carolina and Massachusetts, as so pathetically represented by General Couch. If the one calls out our contempt, the other excites our deepest indignation for its vile hypocrisy, both on the part of its Southern actors and its melodramatic managers from the North.

We have used the term belittleing as the best that could be employed to denote the change that is coming over the character of our great war, and which the necessities of this new reactionary movement demands. It takes the guise of charity, and talks foolishly of "fatted calves." We say, foolishly, for no less irrational than unscriptural is such an application to unrepentant prodigals who demand their portion of goods with more arrogance than when they contemptuously left their father's house. The appeal we make is more especially addressed to our military men. We mean not the mere artificial soldier whose notion of loyalty never rises above the Dalgetty standard—who might as likely have been fighting on the side of the rebellion had it not been for varying circumstances. We had many such men in our army before the war. It was the result of a peculiar training arising out of peculiar circumstances. Even the military oath, ever held so sacred, and which, of all things, it might be supposed, would have made the national predominant over the state or sectional feeling, did not prevent the greater part of them from joining the rebellion. Of those that remained on the national side, some, though they fought well, were just the persons to fall in with these unheroic views of our great struggle, because the side on which they fight does not affect their narrow technical military honor. It was an emblematic loyalty, and they find no difficulty, now that the heat of the strife is over, in prattling chivalry again, and talking of "honorable foes" standing higher in their esteem, perhaps, than the poor southern loyalist, to whom they give no credit for an enthusiastic nationalism which they themselves, it may be, had but little felt. It was only an emblematic loyalty, we say, and they find no difficulty in recognizing a principle equally high with their own, under other emblems than those consecrated to nationality. They would not sing the "bonnie blue flag," but they can hold as chivalrous friends those who do so. It was no feeling of the true heroic, born of unquenchable loyalty to nationalism, that led such men as these, and the course of some of them is now showing it. But they are a small portion even of the regular army, the majority of whom were actuated by a very different spirit, especially as evinced by our two great commanders. Our noble army of Volunteers! the appeal is to you to resist this belittleing process now commenced at Washington, and attempted to be consummated at Philadelphia. *Your* honor—we cannot repeat it too often—*your* honor is at stake. Arouse ye, soldiers of Grant and Sherman, ye men of Fort Donaldson, Vicksburg, and Lookout Mountain. Carry your minds forward to the period when ye shall be old men. Think of your own children asking you about these battle-fields as your fathers inquired of their fathers about Bunker Hill and Saratoga. Do you wish the scenes of peril where you faced death for what you truly felt to be a great cause, and a great question of right, to go down to history with the same lofty remembrance, the same untarnished character of heroism? Then bear in mind that events now passing are to decide, that the present political struggle is to decide, that your votes are to decide, the momentous question in in which you and your children have so deep an interest. Are you at any loss in regard to your ballot, then lay aside all the politician's quibbles about *in* and *out* of the Union, and simply look to movements and tendencies. See in what direction they are hastening. Ask of your own common-sense—with which party, as they are now marshalling, does this great question of the national honor, and of your honor, and of the battle-fields in which you have fought and in which your comrades died, lie most to heart,—to whose keeping their glory may be safely intrusted ? Who make these appeals to you? There is vast significance, we say again, in that. And on which side is there the most cautious reserve if not the most ominous silence, in respect to all that inspired your souls in the hours of danger and of death ? Do you find the ideas and the feelings that then possessed you represented in the Philadelphia-Johnson Convention ? Can you support a movement that calls out the rapturous assent of such unrepentant rebels as Hampton of South Carolina, of Forrest of Fort Pillow, and Monroe of New Orleans? Can you vote just as they would have you ? After all your hard-fought battles, after all your heroic sacrifices, can you be even indifferent to a tendency which, by giving a low character to our national war, can only end by putting Grant on a level with Lee, and Sherman with Hood, and making the dead of Andersonville of no higher account than the drowned pirates of the Alabama ? What would the world have thought; where would have been our remembrances of our fathers if they had proceeded in this manner after our first heroic struggle? Suppose that Tories had been immediately received into Congress, or had even been allowed in some places a greater representation ? Their course was resistance to the establishment of a Republican government when old ideas so strongly led the other way ; the unspeakable atrocity of the Southern conspiracy consisted in its being an attempt to destroy a republican nation after eighty years vigorous life, and the most beneficent rule that earth had ever witnessed. It was a crime which has no parallel in the history of man. Shall these men ever again sit in an American Congress? Shall they make laws, or assist in making laws for you and your children ? This is the great issue of the present canvass. See to it that no foolish cry of "radicalism," no sophims about "policies." and reconstruction, prevent you from looking it steadily in the face. On you, soldiers, above all other men, devolves the duty of so guarding the remembrance of the past five years, that no subsequent events may be allowed to cast the least shadow upon their sublime heroism.

A heroic period, it may be repeated, is one characterized by a predominant unselfishness. The higher attributes of humanity come out, the lower for a season disappear. There may be a counterfeit of this; but the test of its genuineness is the presence and the impulse of a great idea, of a great right, rousing us out of our ordinary indifference. Such was the time through which we have passed. There was romance in it, but romance is not always unreality. The heroic feeling could be seen in the slightest as well as in the greatest events. It poured itself out in national hymns and songs. It had its poetry, some of it poor poetry, indeed, and having all grades of excellence, from the lyre of Whittier to the extemporized ballad of the camp, but all precious as showing the one strong inspiration. It appeared in a hundred ways that at other times we should have regarded as mythical exaggerations. There came again in reality stories that we had heard of only as romantic fictions, or highly colored facts of the older times— mothers offering their children, as had been done in ancient Sparta, and during our first war with Britain,—the wife bidding the husband go forth to the conflict, the maiden, her lover; young children with difficulty restrained at home, and cases not unfrequent of the merest boys falling on the battle-field. Every one must remember how our newspapers abounded in such acoounts—one class of newspapers we mean; for in all this, those that now support "the policy" were as silent as the grave. Exaggeration there may have been in many cases, and yet as a whole falling short of the reality,—assuming the unconscious coloring of the mythical, and yet inadequate as a picture of the truly grand and heroic in the spirit of the times.

This heroic period of ours elevated us by showing us to ourselves in a light we hardly could have imagined before; and now that the scum again is rising, and the vile in politics is coming forth, we are in a condition to measure it by the contrast. Who would have thought ten years ago that such armies could have been raised in such a way, and of such material? But *then* the inspiring, the unselfish idea, had not come, and there was little or nothing in our history for half a century past to aid the imagination in conceiving it. We could not then understand the power of a great and heroic impulse as arising out of a great question touching our national life. We would have deemed it impossible that our old men, our young men, our women, our children, should be possessed by such a spirit, so putting down, and putting out of sight, the ordinary low selfishness of common times. Oh, our heroic boys! Who could have thought it? Never can the writer forget one touching scene in his morning lecture-room. It was in the third year of the war. Many before had gone from the institution; the oldest son of one member of the faculty had given his life early in the conflict; one of its most accomplished Professors had left the college to form a regiment, at whose head he afterward fell in the bloody field of Chancellorville. But there came another call; and on the morning referred to, out of a class-divison of thirty there were eight places silent at the calling of the roll. Their occupants had given their names to a regiment destined for Port Hudson. They endured the severest hardship of the camp and the battle-field as manfully and as cheerfully as they had ever sported on the college green. Some of them never came back. Among these was the prize scholar, the beloved of his class, the only son of his mother. He sleeps by Port Hudson, his grave trampled upon by insolent rebels, but often visited, perhaps, and strewed with flowers and tears by the loyal son of Africa. Oh, those noble boys, worthy of all the renown they had ever read of on the classic page! It comes over me sometimes in a feeling of unbelieving wonder. Were these heroes of the fiercest battle-fields indeed the same young lads whose familiar faces had so often been before me in the lecture-room —those playful boys, so fond of mingling sport with study and whom I had so often chided for their mirth-loving irregularities ! As I think of those young dead faces lying in the trench, or among the blackened ruins of the mine, there comes up a feeling of repentance that, like a croaking senior, I should have ever talked to them of the degeneracy of the age Those noble boys! How soon did the times bring them up not merely to manhood—that false manhood to which we are too apt to hurry in the low selfishness of ordinary life—but to the fullest stature of the most heroic humanity ! From the older graduates of the college more than three hundred went forth, filling all grades, from the general to the private, whilst from larger institutions they mustered in still greater numbers.

And so it was all over the land. But why give these statistics ? What bearing have they on the present political argument ? Much every way. Taken in connection with other facts of a similar kind, they show how much higher a thing than any fictitious romance was the spirit and the solemn verity of the time we call heroic. They show how remarkably the four years, from 1861 to 1865, stand out above all other years in our history, since the period that made us a nation. They excuse us from a formal definition of heroism. We have the thing itself, the fact, before us. They evince how great must have been that question, how lofty that idea, which lifted up the nation to such a hight. But most of all does it show how deeply disastrous, not only to the future political prosperity of our beloved land, but to that higher thing, its spiritual health, is the undervaluing tendency already remarked upon, although it may ever so much take to itself the form of charity, whilst it so utterly ignores that upholding of the right and true which alone can give our commiseration of the vanquished any real or substantial value. But take whatever guise it will, it has always the same unmistakable tendency. Johnson's "swinging round," and Seward's talk of "civil war" and "fatted calves," and Blair's "chivalry," have no other aim nor meaning. The notions that underlie all such affected phraseology, much more the falsehood

that there is in their putting forth, are directly dimming that
high sense of right in which the true heroic has its aliment,
and on the guarding of which the political and the national
well-being so much depends. It is not the North alone that
suffers by it. These things have done, and are now doing,
more to hurt the South than all the suffering caused by Sherman's army, or any subjugation of which the most malignant
copperhead ever dreamed.

Incalculable is the political evil of transforming, in any
way, the character of this glorious period into the reverse
picture of a strife between contending political parties, the
merit or demerit of which is nearly on a par, whose battle-
fields and monumental places are to be regarded as equally
honored, and, therefore, by an inevitable necessity in our
thinking, equally inglorious—such as the whole conflict must
become, on both sides, if these representations be correct—
making us the scoff of the world, and a dishonor among the
nations. The bare statement would seem to be the only argument required. Instead of a traitorous rebellion *subdued*,
with all the legitimate followings of such an act, a mere mis-
understanding, or a factious " civil war," *settled* by an understanding, if not a formal paper treaty,—*no terms imposed, no
rights impaired!* We cannot conceive of anything more disorganizing or *destructive* that could be incorporated into our
history ; and yet the men who favor this would dare to call
themselves Conservatives !

If the view of Seward be correct, then this may be our
first civil war, but it will by no means be our last. If there
be nothing to lift it out of this low category, and put it where
it shall have no future imitation—making it a grand excep-
tional event, with those high marks of difference to which we
have alluded—then may we expect it to be often repeated.·
The example once set of such an attempt, with such an im-
punity, it will come over and over again, as often as favoring
circumstances occur. An assassination, a change of executive, a heavy burthen of debt on the one side, or a capacity

(arising out of a wild state of society) to fight without money or credit on the other, may bring such favoring circumstances sooner than we expect. The thought of a *great right* once gone and the Blair conception taking its place, the true heroic impulse waning and the false chivalry come again, the bright national idea becoming dim and the mischievous league fallacy—such a favorite ever with the smallest of politicians—taking anew possession of the mind,—we may expect our history, in spite of oaths and written constitutions, to be but a repetition of that of the factious States of Greece, and of the Italians of the middle ages.

There is nothing to prevent such a result except the historical hallowing of this time, and setting the brand of everlasting infamy, if not the mark of death and confiscation, on this one desperate attempt at the national life, so excelling in the enormity of its wickedness everything called revolution, civil war, or rebellion in any land less free, less happy than our own. There must be a difference made between our war and all these. Set its glory now so high that it shall be lowered never. Let it be so photographed in the soul of the nation that its bright features shall be never dimmed or lost. Let it be embalmed in the fragrant odors of memory, beyond all reach of harm or decay. This is the present work, demanding no less of struggle, no less of heroism than the war itself. It is this which makes the canvass of 1866 of such incalculable importance. Such is the question, soldiers, to be decided by your ballots, as before by your bullets. Resolve that it shall be decided right, and no further argument need to be addressed to you as to the side on which those ballots shall be cast.

Such a decision we owe to the political virtue of the living. We owe it to the 250,000 dead, the value of whose lives cannot be estimated; for we may safely say that they were among our noblest lives. It was the noblest who were most likely to fall. The brave living who shared their peril will be the last to regard this testimony to their fallen comrades as any disparagement to themselves. 'Twas sung of old by Sophocles—

Πονηρὸν οὐδέν', ἀλλὰ τοὺς Χρηστοὺς ἀεί.
War takes the noblest ever.

In the drama of "Philoctetes," the wounded chieftain on the desert isle is asking news from Troy. Where is Achilles? Dead. And where's Patroclus? Dead. And Ajax, then, and Nestor's noble son Antilochus? All dead and gone.

> PHI. And where's that man of double tongue,
>   Subtle and plausible?
> NEO.   Ulysses lives!
> PHI. Theresites, too? that busy demagogue?
> NEO. They are living still, I hear.
> PHI.   Aye, aye;
>   I do not doubt it. Evil never dies.
>   The fraudful and the vile live on; the brave.
>   They dwell in Hades.

It has a heathen air, but there is a likeness yet in the old poet's limning. Its vivid outlines are still suggestive of men and things near by us. "Subtle and plausible," γλώσσῃ τε δεινὸς καὶ σοφός;—there is no mistaking the modern counterparts. Ajax and Patroclus dead; Ulysses and Thersites still living. The martyr Lincoln slain, the noble Wadsworth lying in his bloody grave; Lyons among the dead,—M'Pherson, Sedgwick, Reynolds, Reno, Mansfield, Kearney, with a host more that would fill pages should we name them,—these all gone; the plotting politicians at Philadelphia sitting in conclave with surviving traitors from the South, the venomous Copperheads, the men of emblematic loyalty, all left behind, to make new compromises, to break the nation's solemn pledge—in a word, to soothe rebellion, and, in so doing, depreciate that high right, that solemn cause of national life for which these glorious heroes fell.

Such depreciation must be the inevitable result of any far-
ther progress in this oblique and downward direction. Already has President Johnson put it out of his power to " make
treason odious," as far as he is concerned. Already has he
put it out of his power to punish it at all, even in its highest
representative. The traitors, indeed, are too numerous to
make the highest punishment of all, by the ordinary process
of law, either possible or desirable ; but events have taken
place that, without change, put it out of the question in respect to every one. The mere pardon, with life and property, given to one distinguished rebel, would not, of itself, be
in the way of the punishment of another ; but to pardon such
a one, with the express purpose of making him governor of a
State, or the mayor of a principal city, and that, too, within a
few months after the laying down of their rebellious arms,
makes all punishment of others impossible, unless all such proceedings are wholly cancelled and reversed. Humphrey in
the gubernatorial chair of Mississippi, Monroe chief magistrate
of New Orleans, Stephens in the Senate, Orr and Wise in
Congress, and Davis on the gallows! Guilty as he is, guilty
as they all are, we could not bear the inconsistency. Some
rebels may be punished whilst some are pardoned ; but we
cannot admit some to seats in Congress and make an example
of any. Such an act of admission is a complete cancelling of
the crime of all. It is equivalent to a solemn decision, that
there is, in fact, no crime in assailing our national life. It is
only a difference of opinion, a viewing things from another
standpoint, and, therefore, perfectly compatible with moral
and political integrity.

A striking illustration of this is furnished by a single
notorious case. There was present as one of the delegates to
the Philadelphia Convention, General Dick Taylor, as he is
called. He, as well as Orr, of South Carolina, was very fond
of the phrase, "fellow-citizens." We know not whether he
has received an official pardon, but it would not have been regarded there as of much consequence, either in excluding or

4

in admitting this *destructive* rebel to that most *conservative* body. He was allowed to come among them and talk of fellow-citizens. Now, this confederate Gen. Taylor, had put to death, at one time, by the most cruel and ignominous mode of hanging, eight "fellow-citizens" of the United States, for no other cause than maintaining that national allegiance which was the direct consequence and duty of their national citizenship. Their alleged crime was nothing else than their loyalty to that government to which he as well as they owed service, and to which he, as a military man, was specially bound by the most solemn superadded and voluntarily assumed oaths. They had enlisted in the Union army, and were thus mercilessly put to death as traitors to a traitorous confederacy, as rebels to a rebellion. Here is a new phase of this atrocious business. Treason itself may be pardoned, rebellion, if it adds no other features, may be amnestied, but a nation that would not avenge its loyal "citizens" thus slain— not slain in battle, but ignominously hung for their loyalty— deserves the world's reproach; it forfeits its national character as a power ordained of God to punish wrong. and vindicate the right. It deserves not that men should be loyal to it; it disowns the allegiance which it pretends to claim, yet cannot, or will not, protect. What hold on Southern loyalty should we have in any future rebellion from the same quarter. No amnesty should have included the perpetrator of this atrocious deed; no special pardon should have extended to *his* treason that mercy which he denied to the loyalty of those brave men. He who hung men for their fidelity to their true allegiance should have felt what was due to a real traitor. Now this man was a delegate to the Philadelphia Convention; his rebel hand, thus foully stained with loyal blood, was grasped by Dix and Custer. He was allowed to say, "fellow-*citizens;*" this murderous *destructive* was cheered in this *conservative* gathering, when he talked of "radicals" and "fanatics." He was there with full credentials, and his reception was an unmistakable sign that his associates in that body deemed him worthy of instant admission into the national legislature, if a majority of rebels like himself had given him their votes for that high place of trust. This mysterious doctrine of "unimpaired State rights," which forms the staple of the Philadelphia reasoning, would make such a man a fit law-maker for the nation whose life he had so assailed, and whose loyal citizens he had thus murdered on the express ground of their loyalty. This was the real "hauling down the national flag," for doing which Gen. Dix would have "instantly" had shot the ignorant Southern soldier who only obeyed the commands of his brutal masters. It saves us another definition. It presents at once the difference between a real and what we have called an emblematic loyalty.

This deed of Taylor's was far from being the only case of the kind. A confederate general in North Carolina hung in one day twenty Union men, and on the same ground of fidelity to the government under which they were born, and to which they owed the highest allegiance. It was not allowed with them to be an "open question." In Texas, too, in East Tennessee, in West Virginia, such tragedies occurred almost daily. The number and names of those who thus suffered will, probably, never be fully known, but certainly there is no matter that more deserves the most searching congressional investigation. And thus does it become one of the great issues of the present political canvass. The *kol dam-im*, the "voice of bloods," if we may use the fearfully intensive Scriptural expression, is crying from the wilds of Texas, and from the mountains of Tennessee. It calls for *vengeance*, not *revenge*, which some are ever confounding with it, but solemn, righteous, judicial investigation with corresponding retribution. Loud is that cry, but God alone will hear it—no national inquiry, no official investigation will be aroused by it, if the government is once wholly surrendered into the hands of the present executive, and his zealous supporters North and South. It will all be left to the "unimpaired rights" of rebellious states. Soldiers of our noble volunteer armies! These loyal men died in their efforts to come to your aid. Can you ever forget them and their yet living suffering compatriots? Your action at the polls must decide that solemn question.

Such cases as these show into what a complication we are brought by the President's most illogical reasonings. If "his policy" is to be continued, he has put it out of his power, and out of the nation's power, to hold to accountability either States or individuals. As far as personal consistency is concerned, he might have held a high theory of State dignity, and yet have vindicated the national justice and the national honor. If they could not rebel as States, if they were ever ideally loyal as States, however strange that might seem in point of fact, then he might have demanded their action against rebellious individuals, and, on failure or refusal, have treated them as mobs and insurrections, or as States under the power of mobs and insurrections, having their forms of government usurped by them, and so constitutionally held them by martial rule (and, in that case, martial protection) until the riotous individuals had all been ejected from their usurped places, the ringleaders judicially treated, and a true loyalty brought out from its idealism into actual and rightful possession of the State power. This would have been the proceeding of a statesman and a patriot, though having a high, and even an excessive, theory of State rights. In this way, too, if patriotism and nationality had been among his controling principles of action, he might have preserved the national honor and the national integrity, as well as his own consistency, to say nothing of fidelity to the great loyal party to whom he was indebted for all his power, whether for good or evil. But there are other considerations, and those, too, consistent with the best aspects of a true States' rights doctrine. If they were real States, such as this theory demands, then they could rebel as States. If they could rebel as States, then they could be punished as States. If they were high corporate persons, owing allegiance as such, then, on the breaking of that allegiance, they could incur forfeitures in the same

41

capacity. This seems to be demanded by the very idea of State dignity. Let us present the only three possible views of State relation. If, in the first place, they were merely municipal districts, greater in jurisdiction, but the same in kind as cities and counties, then the question is easily disposed of. If mobs and insurrections break out in such districts, those mobs may be quelled, their leaders punished, and the district reorganised as expediency and the national will may demand. If, secondly, they are actual sovereignties, bound by an outward league to other sovereignties, then, on their breaking that league, they may be either let go, or they may be coerced to its observance. This would follow even on the extreme Calhoun doctrine; but even then this ultra theory of leagued sovereignties, false as it is, would not warrant the absurd Philadelphia platform. On coercion for breaking their contract, or treaty with other sovereignties, they are not brought back to its observance with "unimpaired rights," but with such new terms and new conditions as the laws of war and of nations allow to be imposed. They may be required to pay the expenses of the war; there may be demanded of them the banishment of individuals; they may be even declared annexed or conquered. But if, *thirdly*, what we call States are somewhere between these two extreme views, then are they, at the highest, political personalities, not simply bound by a league to, but owing, in common with others, a true allegiance to, a higher political personality, which is not a mere *aggregate* of these lower corporations, but a true historical being, of which they are the organization, or the form, but not the organizing power;—that organizing power residing in a "people" or nationality lying back of all, and making a sovereignty not simply over States, and claiming allegiance merely from States as such, but over all individuals in those States, and claiming allegiance from every man of them in the exercise of all those powers to which such whole people or nationality has constitutionally *limited itself*, and which it may *constitutionally* diminish or enlarge. Still, by such organization as aforesaid, the underlying States may be regarded as political personalities, thus distinguished from mere municipal districts on the one hand, or leagued sovereignties on the other. This is *our* State system, or form of national organization. If, however, they are thus restricted political personalities, then they, too, as such political corporations, owe a true allegiance to the higher national personality as well as the individual personalities of whom they are composed. All allegiance implies accountability, with liability to penalty and forfeiture for its breach. Otherwise we run into the utter political absurdity that the parts of a nation, whether individual or corporate persons, may be guilty of any disorder, endangering the life of the whole, and, on the forcible quelling of such disorder, relapse immediately into their former state, with no rights impaired, repelling every remedial method made necessary by such disorder, and treating as a wrong the demand of any security against future danger, except their own assertion, however made, that, for the present, they resist no more. In such a case the seeming coercion is, in fact, non-coercion; it is not carried out; nothing is effected by it; it had better never have been begun; if accompanied by a great sacrifice of life, it is a folly and a crime.

It all amounts, then, to this : If they are corporate persons they have corporate liabilities. As said before, the very dignity of the State idea, if it have any dignity, demands this. If so, then they may commit treason, which is, in its essence, a violation of allegiance. If they could commit treason, then they could incur, and did incur, the forfeitures and consequences of treason, although their corporate being rendered them incapable of suffering some of its specific penalties as they may be inflicted on individuals. Civil death is one of these consequences of treason, whether as committed by individuals or corporations. It is, in fact, both a penalty and a consequence. Such civil death results directly from the idea of breach of allegiance, as separation from a common national life. This can happen to States. If they cannot be hung by the neck like individual traitors, their political life may be *sus-*

pended, and is of itself suspended, by the very act of treason—that is, the withdrawal of allegiance. If, then, this political life comes into them again, it must be from the action of the great national body in which, as a whole, the life still remains unimpaired in the fountain and principle of its vitality, and which, as before proved, is pre-eminently represented in the great national Legislature.

We hope the reader will pardon this dry argumentation. The great principle for which we contend could not well be set forth in briefer or less abstract terms. But waiving all this, and supposing that the President, for any reason, could not see his way in this direction, then he had a clear course in the other. Taking his own theory, so inconsistent with his other notions of State power and State dignity, so inconsistent, too, with actual facts, namely, that no action of a State could affect its relation to the Union—that it was never *out*, however solemnly it had declared itself to be *out*—that it had never, as a State, made war upon the nation, however explicitly and in all its corporate action, legislative, judicial, and conventional, it had declared and carried on such war—suppose we admit that *as States* they ever continued, regularly and harmoniously, in all their rights and relations to the Union, and that all that took place were the acts of mobs and insurrections under which those ever loyal States were suffering, even as Massachusetts, to which the President so illogically compared them, suffered from Shay's rebellion—suppose, I say, we admit all this, strange as it seems, and allow that everything done was done by individuals with only individual liabilities, although these individuals comprised all the governors, all the judges, all the legislators, all persons holding positions in the organic machinery of these strange nondescript bodies—what then? Why, surely, as " treason *must* be made odious," these individuals, or at least the worst among them, should have been held liable for treason. They should have been reached in some way, and if this could not have been done through the State organizations, or through the judiciary therein (whether called State or National), on account of sympathy with them, then they should have been treated as mobs still, and other and loyal organizations put in their places. The whole of the President's difficulty is solved by the plain distinction, before made, between the *Nation* and the *Union* as the form of its organization. It is also disposed of by the unanswerable argument drawn from the fact that each one of the rebellious States had broken its own constitution, if it be a sound principle that the national constitution is a part, and an essential part, of the constitution of each State. But waiving all this, we say again, why not proceed against them as individuals—why not, in some way, "make treason odious?" Now here presents itself again the strange complication that comes directly from these illogical ideas. It is the monstrous shifting of responsibility till it lodges no where, and no body can be touched. Were these States all this time, full, lawful States, or lawless mobs? They must not be *States* for one purpose and *mobs* for another—mobs when the attempt is made to hold the State to its forfeitures and its liabilities, and then States again when the individual actors in these mobs and insurrections want to interpose State authority and State allegiance as their shield. It was supposed that though it might be false there was really some dignity in this doctrine of State rights, so that a man might hold it and yet have some claim to reason and respectability. It was thought there was some chivalry about it, but as thus used, what a miserable skulking thing it is! Look at the pitiable position of Alexander H. Stephens. Do you hold, sir, that the State of Georgia was out of the Union? By no means, is the reply. The State could not be legally out of the Union, and, therefore, it was not out of the Union. What a sudden conversion this, of these once nation-reviling conspirators, to the new Johnsonian doctrine! But who made the war then? As the State could not be legally out of the Union, and must therefore, be supposed to have maintained unimpaired its loyal relations to the Union, the irregularities referred to can only be regarded as the unauthorized acts of mobs or individuals. Very well, sir, but now another question. Were you, as an individual, guilty of treason? Not at all. The State of Georgia held to the right of secession; its inhabitants, including myself, still hold to it, although we do not mean to assert it just now, and what I did was by virtue of my allegiance to a sovereign State. It was therefore not treason against the United States. Who can understand it? The representation, so far as it can be put into words at all, would seem to be something like this. Back of all the mobs and turbulence stands the ideal State as fair as ever. *Actually*, its governor is the head of a most violent insurrection against the national authority; *ideally* he is head of a political body the harmony of whose relations to the great republic has never been impaired, and which holds its place the same, at all times, without terms or conditions. But are you and others then, guilty of treason? In answer to this question, there instantly vanishes the mob which had so strangely represented this abstract corporation. The State itself now emerges from its idealism, and under it the mob and all the actors in the mob, from Vice-President Stephens down, immediately take shelter. Shall a great nation be juggled in this way? Shall a quarter of a million of our noblest men have died and no other result come from it than such a thimble-rigging farce as this! The cruelties of Andersonville shock us more, but the pain they occasion is less than the feeling that hence arises, of our utter national humiliation.

This complication is coming widely into view, and bids fair, unless soon untied, to make infinite confusion in future judicial proceedings. Take again the case of Dick Taylor aforesaid, or that of the North Carolina general, who hung twenty loyal Union men. Suppose these persons indicted for murder, to say nothing of the crime of treason. The blood they have thus shed cries to heaven, and orphan children are asking justice against the slayers of their innocent parents. There is the form of an arraignment, when lo! there is pro-

duced on the trial, the orders of a confederate governor, or
the warrant of a confederate general, and all this sanctioned
by confederate sovereign States, whose acts, during all the
time of the rebellion, must be held to be as legitimate as before and after; for they were never out of the Union, and
their rights in it were never in the least impaired. Add to
this the doctrine of Judge Ruffin, lately ratified by a popular
vote in North Carolina, that no acts, or conventions, or proceedings of any kind, that were forced upon them by military
or any outside authority have any validity, and we have a
state of political confusion unexampled in the annals of the
world. If they were simply mobs and insurrections, then
Gen. Lee, and every man in his army, were each liable to in-
dictment of murder for every Union soldier slain, of arson for
every building burned, of robbery for every article of property
taken or destroyed. But who expects them ever to be found
guilty on any such indictments, or to be punished in any way,
if the President's policy is carried out, and this mysterious
doctrine of State rights is allowed to shift from the actual to
the ideal, or from the ideal to the actual, in any way that may
be required to shield crime on the one hand, or to get rebels
into Congress on the other? The pleas of which we speak
have been already offered and received in Southern courts.
Many more such will be offered, and the result will be that
by means of this wretched juggle, no man however guilty will
be punished; no man as well as no State will find any rights
impaired, or any wrongs imputed whatever crimes he may
have committed.

Now, aside from the political inconsistency, such a state of
things as this is most demoralizing. It is a shocking, and a
consequent benumbing, of the national conscience. The health-
ful preservation of the great ideas of right and wrong, of the
eternal distinction between truth and falsehood, of the sanctity
of the national oath, of the feeling that such a great right and
truth were involved in our national struggle, is a higher thing,
a more precious thing, than any amount of sentimental con-

ciliation, whatever guise of charity it may assume. The moral sense is hurt, and, in time, becomes diseased, by the sight of guilt, especially great guilt, going about unpunished. This is, in fact, the ultimate ground of punishment in human law as representative of the divine. It is deeper than all the policies and expediencies that are usually urged as the only penal sanction. Call penal justice utilitarian if you will, but then the production and preservation of a healthy social conscience is the highest earthly utility. Guilt unpunished is ever demoralizing. It is still more demoralizing when some punishments are inflicted, but with that gross inequality which shocks instead of admonishing. When, for example, a miserable Clamp Ferguson writhes upon the gallows as a guerrilla, whilst his clerical instructor in rebellion is admitted into Christian pulpits, and his 'military commanders, whom he thought he was zealously serving in his irregular mode of war, are lionized at Philadelphia conventions; or when the poor, stolid, brutal-tempered Wirtz is executed for crimes almost forced upon him by his position, whilst men who placed him there, and kept him there, are regarded as eligible to Congress, and the right of rebellious States to send them there is pronounced unbroken and "unimpaired."

It is a plea often used in palliation of Southern treason, that they were " *educated* " in the doctrine of State sovereignty, and that they should, therefore, be judged from this their own " stand-point." The answer to it is, that the men for whom such plea is specially made were not so much the *educated* in this idea as they were themselves the *educators*. It might have some force as offered for that debased class commonly called the " poor whites;" but it is a mean hypocrisy when used in behalf of such men as Stephens, Wise, and Orr. For long years had they directed all their efforts to instill this political poison into the Southern mind. Secession, and the extreme State rights doctrine out of which it arose, is not a natural American growth either North or South. Born of Southern sectionalism, even as that was born of the exotic slavery, it took long years, and the favoring fact of a peculiarly ignorant population, to make it grow. The national idea, on the other hand, was the true American plant. It showed itself as an organizing power, even before our history had shaped the nation into its more regular growth and form. It was born of our Anglo-Saxon nationality. We see its progress, drawing the wide-sparse districts closer together, in the French and Indian wars, in the early American Congresses, and in other acts that preceded the revolution. These were emphatically American Congresses, for they showed the germinal nation, even before the umbilical cord was severed that bound us to our historic mother. For the preservation of this, as much as for separation from Great Britain, was the battle fought. It was never meant to lose that binding idea, the want of which would have rendered the struggle, in other respects, a mischief instead of a blessing. The parts were acknowledged, but that only rendered all the more precious that from which these rights of the parts have all their meaning. It was those most precious "State rights" which the demagogue does not understand, or undervalues for the mere petty local power, to which alone he gives the name. It was that higher right of every colony, of every State, and of the people of every State, in every other State,—that right of unimpaired citizenship throughout the wide Anglo-Saxon American territory. It was this, too, or its more perfect security, for which the Constitution of 1787 was formed. The great thing wanted was the more perfect equalization everywhere of the valuable and acknowledged rights of every part in every part, and in the whole, so that there might be no local legislation on matters in which all had an interest, or that would make a man less a man, less a citizen, with less of the rights of a citizen, in one portion than in another. These higher State rights demanded a general guardianship against the narrow, local, sectionalizing State rights doctrine which, while jealous for the corporate, is most likely to be regardless of the individual liberty. We see this plainly now—how much more favorable to the individual freedom is the larger jurisdiction, and how it has to struggle to preserve it against the local power.* If conservatism is the standing firm, by the fundamental and distinguishing idea of a government, then he among us is the true conservative who is the most national, and, at the same time,

---

* This may be made clear by a brief analysis. In our beautiful yet complicated structure of government there arise five species of rights. 1st, the rights of the nation; 2d, the rights of the States in the nation; 3d, the rights of the States in each other; 4th, the rights of the States in their local jurisdictions; 5th, last of all, yet the most precious of all, or that for which all the rest exist, the right of the individual in the State, in the nation, and in both to be unhindered in the attainment of any place, franchise, or benefit which the powers that God has given him may enable him to attain, and on the same terms, be they high or low, and on the same conditions on which they are allowed to be attained by any other individual in the State, or in the nation; in other words, perfect political equality.

It is certainly a remarkable fact, that whilst in the republican strivings in Europe the tendency is strongly toward such acknowledgment of the rights of the individual, as the ultimate political aim, here, on the other hand, there are held doctrines, and those, too, called democratic, which tend directly the other way, making the preservation of certain corporate rights a higher thing (a more democratic thing they would say) than the very end for which those corporations have any value. Attorney-General Speed, in his paper of resignation, admirably presented this idea of the higher value of the individual right; and it is to be hoped that a thought so old, and yet so new, may become a leading principle in our politics, not to be put out by any efforts of a false democracy.

The common, noisy, undefined, and incapable-of-being-defined States rights doctrine stands equally opposed to the rights of the nation and the rights of the individual. This comes from an instinctive conviction on the part of its advocates that the broad shield of the one is the great security of the other, as against local tyranny or local prejudice; and that in a republican land, what they call centralization is the very reverse of what goes under the same name in a despotism; that it is, in fact, the diffusing power, the equalizing power sending out liberty and securing liberty to every part. Hence their, evil jealousy and their false logic; hence, too, their utterly undemocratic position.

most strenuous for individual rights. Never was there a greater anomaly presented in the history of political philosophy than the manner in which, through the abused name of *centralization*—totally misapplied from its French or European use—the lower has tended to displace the higher, and the petty claims of locality, or of indefinable corporate abstractions, have been urged to the damage of the RIGHTS OF THE STATES in each other. Among these is the interest of each State in the institutions of every other, and the corresponding right to demand that those institutions be equal and republican. It was for this, and to secure the rights of individuals, both in the States respectively and in the whole, that the present Constitution was solemnly ordained by, and in the name of THE PEOPLE OF THE UNITED STATES.

This is the true *Conservatism*. It is the reverse doctrine that is *destructive* of our fundamental national idea. The "endangered liberties of the States"—this cry of the demagogue has come to mean little else than the liberty of trampling upon liberty, or the liberties of oligarchical States to infringe upon the liberties of individuals, and, in so doing, to make war upon the most precious *liberties* of other States, as well as upon the most sacred *rights* of the nation. But, whatever be the nature of this doctrine of State sovereignty, these men for whom it is now plead as a palliation were themselves its teachers. *They* were the educators. They controlled Legislatures and Conventions by it. The ignorant rebellious communities which they had thus educated obeyed them, instead of their obeying their States. The plea, we say, might do for the deluded masses whom they pressed into their armies; but how utterly false and base it is when made by such men as Stephens, Wise, and Lee, or when they suffer their friends at Philadelphia to make it for them.

Mobs to go out, and States to come back.

States to go out, and mobs to come back—

Take it either way you please, according as the application or the purpose demands. We have already remarked upon some of these. In the case of Mr. Alex. H. Stephens, this double-headed monstrosity goes both ways at once. It might be treated as a political farce were it not for some awfully serious questions to which it gives rise. Among these there is none of deeper interest, or more directly entering into the present canvass, than that which relates to the future fate of the Southern loyalists. They have been resisting mobs, for which, it was supposed, they deserved the gratitude and protection of the nation; but, lo! this mob suddenly presents itself as the State, the strange ideal State which has been existing all the time, and, now, according to the Philadelphia doctrine, comes forth with all its rights unimpaired, among which is the absolute right to legislate for all people within its territory,—to punish, banish, ostracise, or disfranchise for any crime it may invent, or any cause it may allege. This is one of its reserved inherent sovereign rights. There is, indeed, an act of Congress, called the Civil Rights Bill, which might seem to be in the way, but that is everywhere pronounced unconstitutional in Southern courts, and the Executive is in deadly hostility to it. What is to protect these men? Their case is unexampled. The nation has triumphed, it is said; and yet they are worse off than if they had been disloyal. There is something else in their condition more marvellous still. The complication into which the President's policy has brought the whole affair makes their situation actually more helpless and deplorable than though the nation had been defeated and the rebellion had triumphed in the field. This may seem a strange assertion, and we therefore proceed to prove it. In doing so, let us call up a fact now fifty years past in the history of our relations to a foreign Government. In the negotiations between the United States and Great Britain, at the close of the war of 1812, the latter made the protection of their Indian allies a matter of most express stipulation. Other things were earnestly insisted upon, offered and rejected, pressed at one time and yielded at another by both parties, but from this demand the British Government never would recede. It was with them more than a matter of interest or policy. Their national honor was at stake; the world's eye was upon them; they thought how they would look in history, and they made it a *sine qua non.* These Indian allies lived in the then wilderness territories of Michigan and Wisconsin. Our Government had claimed from them a quasi allegiance, but this was certainly something far less than the allegiance which bound to it Southern men, rebels or loyalists, in 1861. They had aided Britain in her war, and she would not abandon them to our "unimpaired" jurisdiction without the fullest assurance, accompanied by positive security for their protection. Whatever we may think of that war, or however we may dislike the English nation, their conduct in this respect was just and noble. And now, how utterly reversed is our course, if the Johnson policy is to prevail, and that, too, not with Indians having, perhaps, a doubtful claim, but with men, citizens of the United States, distinguished above all for their loyalty and their sufferings. To make this clear let us picture in imagination a state of things which, three or four years ago, was far from being impossible, or even improbable. There were times in our great struggle when the boldest hearts grew faint. It did seem, sometimes, as though the great point would have to be conceded, and the Southern secession acknowledged. In such a case we could not have abandoned these Southern loyalists. The world would have cried out against us. Though yielding other things, here we must have insisted to the last; and, for the sake of acknowledged independence, the South would, doubtless, have accepted the terms, and given such security, whether by way of territorial hostage or otherwise, as would have been, by the law of nations, an adequate protection against all liability or deprivation of rights. Bitterness, it may be, would have existed against them, but the dread of another war, which we could not have refused to wage on violation of such a treaty, would have secured quiet and tolerance, even a tolerance which the transactions at Memphis and New Orleans show to be now

unknown. How strange the spectacle! How astounding
the paradox which we now present, especially to the lovers
of freedom abroad, and which comes directly from this most
unheard-of "policy," and this most mysterious doctrine of
"unimpaired State rights." Our national armies triumphant,
rebellion subdued, the loyal North rejoicing, the loyal men
of the South expecting, beyond all others, to share in
that joy, and to partake of the benefit, even as beyond all
others they had shared in the suffering—the President of the
nation belonging to this very class—and yet, after all, left in
a worse condition than though the rebellion had been successful—left in a position where every feeling is embittered
against them, and yet without the security that would have
come from a treaty, without the security that Great Britain
insisted upon for her Indian allies! What the horrors of that
position actually are late events have shown beyond a doubt.
In Louisiana more union-men slain in one day of peace (so
called) than during the whole four years of unrelenting war!
And what is to come? What is to set any check upon this
Philadelphia doctrine of State rights unimpaired. They may
make any exclusions, any disfranchisements they please of
these suffering loyalists. They may interdict to them any
social or political assemblings. They can persecute them in
innumerable ways. They can consign them to civil death,
and put it into their constitutions. They can banish them as
enemies of the State, and there is no power on earth that can
forbid any such proceedings. Citizenship of the United States
cannot protect them, for the President holds that there is no such
citizenship aside from that of the States; and we are reasoning
now on the inevitable consequences of his policy if sanctioned
by the nation at the ballot-box. And here comes up another
monstrous anomaly, which is a legitimate result of that most
unheard-of policy. We fought four years, lost 250,000
lives, and incurred a burthen of 3,000,000,000 dollars of debt,
to vindicate our claim to be a nation; and yet citizenship,
ever held to be inseparable from nationality, is declared by

our President not to belong to it. It pertains alone to the
States. A nation without citizens, and without power to protect them if it had any! Such are the doctrines of "the
policy." Such is one of the momentous questions to be decided by the present canvass. Can it be that any loyal man
at the North shall regard this as the true reconstruction of the
Union after such a war? Can it be that the soldiers of our
noble armies, and to such throughout this appeal we have
especially addressed ourselves—can it be that any who fought
under Grant, and followed Sherman through the South, can
misunderstand an issue so nearly affecting the national honor
and their honor, knowing as they do what these Southern
allies of theirs endured, and at what a price their loyalty was
maintained? It must not be, it cannot be, that a nation
which has lost 250,000 lives in maintaining its nationality
should be unable to protect its humblest citizens, much less
those who are placed in positions of suffering and persecution
from their devotion to it in its hour of sorest trial.

"Sneaks" is the name which the Johnson newspapers are
giving to these crushed men, and copperheads throughout the
land are reiterating it. "Recreants" Blair calls them—recreants to their *own side*. Can you bear this, soldiers? You
see in it the progress of the new idea the President has intro-
duced, and which becomes necessary for the support of his
policy. There might have been some plausibility in it if
indeed it had been a question of *sides* or localities instead of
that high issue which we have endeavored to keep prominent
in all that we have said—not a war of the North against the
South, nor of factions "swinging round," nor a "civil war," as
Seward calls it, but the nation against assassins that sought
its life—the whole nation, politically, against traitorous foes
more hostile and more alien to it than any foreign enemies.
This utter debasing of the whole matter to a thing of locality
casts dishonor upon you as well as upon the suffering men to
whom these epithets are applied. *Your* nationality was *their*
nationality. Your love of country, and of her glorious insti-

tutions of freedom, was their love of country, only the more severely tested by the counter-strength of the narrower local feeling, and of the persecutions to which they were exposed.

Thus, whatever view we take, whatever seemingly collateral point may call attention, the same great issue is ever coming up again. Through all complications it ever stands before us. The conflict is not over, soldiers! You conquered at Gettysburg, at Richmond, and New Orleans. There is yet to be won another battle which is to prevent all your former triumphs from having been in vain. The question now to be decided is the glory of the cause in which you fought. A mean reaction is seeking to lower it, in its attempts to rescue from deserved odium the men who have caused all our national woe. They are attempting to revive the old pernicious doctrines in which secession had its birth. A false "policy" finds itself driven to such a course in its own defense. A false demoralizing sentimentality is undermining the higher and healthier ideas of *truth* and *right*. To the same end, and with a similar demoralizing effect, an emblematic loyalty is talking again of "chivalry," and "honorable foes," whilst offending the moral sense of all Christendom in its treachery to Southern loyalists, and its base abandonment of that crushed race whose aid we sought in the hour of our greatest danger. Influences like these may draw with them some few who were once esteemed patriotic, but the masses in the opposing ranks are still the same old elements of disloyalty. They are the men who were the soldiers' foes, and the foes of his cause, during all the anxious years of the conflict.

Not platforms then, as we have before remarked, but movements, tendencies, and affinities, unerring and unmistakable, are the things to which, as men of common sense, as wise men, we are to look. A few questions, which it requires only a moment's honest thinking to answer, settle all: What side is sure to receive the vote of every warmest sympathizer with

rebellion in our land? On which side will be found the men
who rejoiced—and their name is legion—at defeats in our
armies? In whose success will *they* feel deepest interest who
had no tears for our gallant dead, and who stigmatized then,
as some others are doing now, the war in which they fell as
fanatical, false, and inglorious? Where will *they* vote who
were ever against giving the right of voting to the absent
soldier in the camp? Where will deserters vote, and they
who are striving to get repealed, or declared unconstitutional
by the courts, the laws by which such deserters were right-
eously disfranchised? On which side will success give most
joy in Charleston and New Orleans? Whose triumph will
cause mourning to every liberty-loving republican of Europe,
and rejoicing to every liberty-hating partisan of monarchy and
aristocracy. Soldiers of Grant and Sherman—if these questions can be answered in but one way—and you most surely
know what *that* is—how can any of you vote on a side which
will inevitably bring you into association with every one of
these.

Never was issue more sharply joined. It is not so much
the particular names of candidates, or even the measures, however plausibly stated, of which they profess to be the advocates, as the influences that support them, and which will be
the controlling power in spite of all professions. Via media
men, third party men, ever, with all their claims to conservatism, the most factious, mischief-making men in a nation, may
profess what they please, but that which is most powerful and
most numerous in the voting ranks will not only be predominant, but claim full recognition of its predominance, in case of
success. And we all know what that ruling interest is, and of
what elements it is composed. All that is most hostile to our
true nationality, is there. All the most extreme advocates of
the baleful doctrine of State sovereignty are there. Every one
among us who was a member of a secret society in aid of
Southern treason is there. Every one who is engaged in the

ineffably vile work of creating a new sectionalism between the East and the West—every such man is there. All who are distinguished by the most demoniac feeling toward a crushed and disfranchised race are there. All who call the loyalists of Louisiana and East Tennessee, " sneaks " and " recreants " are there. They are all there. Soldier, patriot, can you vote with them?

In order to lift themselves out of the deserved degradation into which they have heretofore fallen, all these classes are seeking to depreciate the character of our late war. They would send it down in history, inglorious and dishonored. They would put a stigma upon those who have been its most zealous supporters. In other words, they would in every way lower the standard of the national cause. Soldiers, be it yours to set it high, to put the emblematic symbol of its honor where no hand can ever " haul it down." Looking away then from all complications, from all " policies "—keeping the eye steadily fixed on unmistakable tendencies and results—make to yourselves these firm resolves : This struggle shall not have been in vain ; its deep grounds of righteousness shall not be undervalued, and its most loyal supporters reviled, that rebels may be relieved from deserved ignominy ; such an immense sacrifice of life shall not have been made merely that they may come back again to their abandoned seats in Congress, and even with an increased representation ; such hosts of our comrades shall not have fallen that there may be, in the rebellious States, less freedom of speech, less unhindered political action, less protection to individual rights, than there was before. It shall not be that the brave Southern loyalists, given up to the " unimpaired rights " of such rebellious jurisdictions, should be in a worse condition than though they had been disloyal—in a worse condition even than if the rebellion had never been subdued. Above all, soldiers—in no unchristian temper of vain chivalrous boasting, but with a sober regard to the future spiritual and political health of the land in which your children are to live—say with one voice: The standard we have borne aloft through so many battle-fields, it shall not be lowered—the historic glory of this our second heroic period, of this our second great war for nationality—IT MUST, IT SHALL BE PRESERVED.

www.ingramcontent.com/pod-product-compliance
Lightning Source LLC
Chambersburg PA
CBHW021638270326
41931CB00008B/1071